JUST WORDS
ON A PAGE

JUST WORDS
ON A PAGE

LYNETTE COLLINS

Rev. date: 09/08/2016

To order additional copies of this book, contact:
Xlibris
1-800-455-039
www.Xlibris.com.au
Orders@Xlibris.com.au
748556

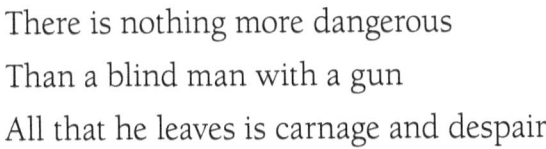

There is nothing more dangerous
Than a blind man with a gun
All that he leaves is carnage and despair

It is easy to say yes
When you know you should say no
When fear is the gun that is pointed at you

JUST WORDS ON A PAGE

When the choices we make
Are our only crime
Those who judge us
Live with a closed mind

Prejudice
For prejudice does not care for the colour
of skin on which it dwells,
It strikes for free by planting the seed of hate.

His heart lived alone
His mind lived with millions

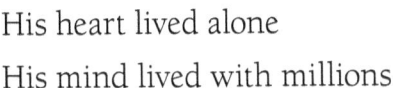

You cannot get the rainbow,
Without, a little rain

If they are her thoughts
Why didn't she press print?

I planted a seed
I called it faith
A flower grew from it
I looked the next spring
There was a garden of love
I called it my future

JUST WORDS ON A PAGE

Insanity is when somebody else is writing
Their words over or on top of your thoughts

They imprison a man for his words of wisdom
And he frees a nation with the strength
That comes from his convictions.

JUST WORDS ON A PAGE

For you do not have the right
To place judgement on any one else
When you are looking through
The windows of hate

One cannot know the value of one's true self
If deception is the gift they give to others

JUST WORDS ON A PAGE

If pity is all you know
Then entitlement becomes
Your ambition

Their jealousy is what ties them together
Their respect is what will untie the knot

The lies you try to hide
Becomes the truth in other's eyes
Until you have to pick a side

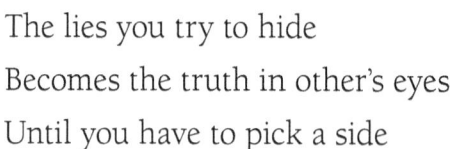

You can only see hate
When you are looking
Through jealous eyes

I cannot hear your hateful words
For I am deaf to negative people

For if you can only see my mistakes
Then you are trapped in the past
And I live in the future
Where I am free

For understanding is the key
To moving on and being free

It is his honesty that defines him
So he can live with open eyes

JUST WORDS ON A PAGE

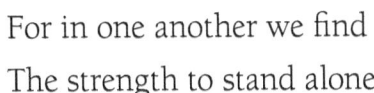

For in one another we find
The strength to stand alone

For our body can be homeless
But our soul lives in a castle
And is free

For do not punish the ones I love
For the judgement you have placed
Upon me

For our entitlements can become
Our disease that binds us to others
And stops us from becoming who we should be
Instead who they think we can be

12

For the devil hides in all of us
But for some they give him the key

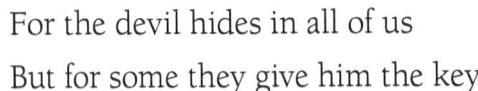

For when they choose the devil
Their future dies
He gives them your soul
That is why they have to lie

For your door is made of gold
And the key is in your sight

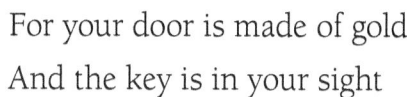

For evil is blind
It can only hear
That is why
Silent is so feared

For in her haze to take my freedom
　　She imprisons herself
　　And all her weak men

For if I judge people
On what they look like
I would be judging myself
With blind eyes

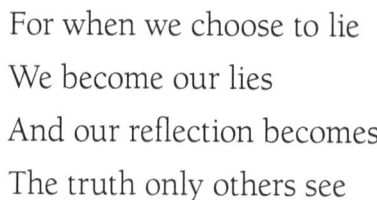

For when we choose to lie
We become our lies
And our reflection becomes
The truth only others see

Where there is peace
The heart you see
Is of fullness and is complete

To build a bridge takes time
To build it with love
Will cost you nothing
The only thing that will break it
Will be your dishonesty

When the light is shining on us
We glow with beauty
It is when it has been turned off
That we see who we truly are

JUST WORDS ON A PAGE

For you cannot
Imprison me with your lies
For my mind sees the truth
For my soul sets me free
And she has the key to my mind
And only she knows where she hides it

For if you only pick the painting
For its pretty colours
It becomes a painting on the wall
But if you pick the painting
For the story it is telling you
It becomes the centre piece
Of the room

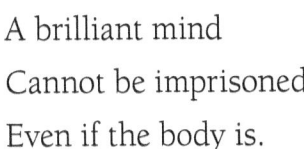

A brilliant mind
Cannot be imprisoned
Even if the body is.

Offered opinions may be different to yours
But are of no less value to the world

You cannot dictate my mind
On who I am to become
For I was born with my own destiny
And it is him I shall follow.

When your reflection
Is the only one you see?
The only love you receive
Is your own

In your eyes I see a reflection
Of you
Where money has no value
Only time

When you work more than you rested
Money becomes your master
And he is the only one that is missed

When winning is all that matters
In the game you love
Then you have already lost
Before the game has even started

You will never find fulfilment in another
Rather only happiness when they are near

You do not become
A part of someone else
When you are in a relationship
Rather they become an extension
Of your happiness

If we talked as much about
The things that make us happy
And less about the things
That make us unhappy
The conversation would last longer
And more people would want to join in

JUST WORDS ON A PAGE

When you look through closed eyes
Then that is when the best
Part of who you are
Is left in the darkness

He thought for what he believed in
With a peaceful army
And they changed the world
With their actions

JUST WORDS ON A PAGE

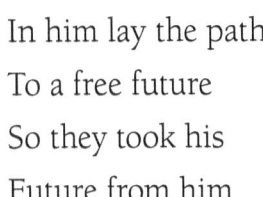

In him lay the path
To a free future
So they took his
Future from him

She changed herself to please others
Then tried to find herself within them
But they did not know who
They were looking for

He became a rebel for he thought
He was of more greatness than this world
And now his name is all that the world
Knows about him

When we fall from the top it is okay
For when we start our journey back up
We know all the short cuts
And the journey does not take as long

The second time we do things
Is always better than the first
For we have become
The instruction book

They have enough money to feed the world
And with their money they starve themselves

He lived a life of fantasy
And in his fantasy
He found the truth
He gave it to the world
And in return for his gift
We placed judgement on him

He gave the boy a lifetime of happiness
And as he lay dying
The tear fell from the boy's eyes
And on to his face
And in that moment he knew
His life was of value

He took everything he wanted
And still he died alone

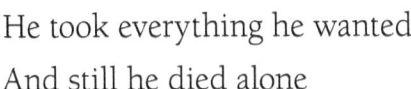

I cried not for what she had done to me
But for her regret was so overwhelming

When you try to walk in someone else's shoes
Remember the soles in the shoes
Has been worn in to suit only their footsteps

As I look and roll my eyes
I understand her more now
Now I am looking through
My mother's eyes

JUST WORDS ON A PAGE

For I never want to be you
For I like who I am too much

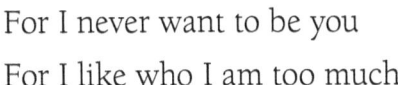

For watch the road you are travelling on
And not mine
For my eyes do not leave the road
Nor the light that is my destiny

For I am patient in finishing my dreams

For my dreams wait for me

For I do not mind if I am forgotten

For it is my truth I want to be remembered

Never give your dignity to another

For when they leave they take it with them

Wisdom is given to those who listen
Not to those who think
They already know everything

For your wisdom is a gift my soul
Accepts from you
And shares it with my mind

It is hard to close the door to hate
When hate keeps opening it up again

For lost is who you are today,
But found is who you will be tomorrow,
But forgotten is who you will never be,
For the memory of you,
Will always live through me.

You will know when you have truly loved someone,
From when they are no longer in your life,
You will miss the things you did for them,
Rather than the things they did for you.

I listen to everything people say to me,
But I choose not to comment
On everything I hear.

I tried to live my life without sin, for sin opens the door to shame,

And with shame I would walk looking at the ground,

And I would much rather be looking at the beautiful faces of others.